Let's Talk About Money

The Guide to Not Being Poor.

By: Will Holmes

Dedication

This book is dedicated to all my mentors and teachers who made sure I was aware of how the world works. Did you know it works because money makes it work? That's some pretty crazy stuff.

Specifically, I wanted to thank my parents, grandfather and both Dave Ramsay and Robert Kiyosaki. Thank you all for your teaching.

Table of Contents

Introduction

Ever since I can remember I have always wanted to be wealthy, and I don't just mean fancy cars, a nice house, and a private jet rich, what I wanted is much, much more than that. I wanted to be so wealthy that no generation that comes after me will ever have to work a day in their lives (if they didn’t want to). I wanted to be so wealthy that there was no experience or thing that I couldn’t afford. Wouldn’t the ability to not care about how much something costs be great? Wouldn’t it be amazing never to have to worry about money? All those wishes are attainable and not are they possible for me, but they are possible for anyone, but in order to really start to tackle those objectives we need to know the rules of the game of wealth. Now would also be a good time to mention that (for legal reasons) this is not official financial advice. #don’t sue me. Additionally, all the data (such as interest rates) are used at the time of writing this book (unless specified otherwise). With that said and the disclaimer out of the way, let’s journey back in time to see how historical events have impacted the modern financial environment. Lastly, I realize finance books are usually “totally lame” and boring because finance *can* be a rather dry topic. So, I’ll try not to be too boring or dry. So, let's move this along and talk about our first real topic.

How Did We Get Where We Are Today?

The year is 2008, the day September 29th, and global finance as we know it is about to completely collapse. The world is currently within twenty-four hours of ATM(s) running dry, and while many financial and real estate people like Grant Cardone will say "cash is trash" on 9/29/08, cash could not have been more "the king".

Nowadays we all focus heavily on the stock market crash and then recession of 2008, but the underlying issue highlighted by the stock market crash of September 29th, 2008, is not a unique problem. In fact, the underlying issue is one that has caused many market crashes before…however as many financial experts will attest, people are not very good at learning from their mistakes…especially when the idea of "free money" (i.e., leverage) arises. Both the U.S. and the global economy are in a recession right now (as of writing this), and although the root cause of this recession is slightly different, it is the same underlying principle that is creating a "great and global recession". With that said, what we all need to acknowledge is that instead of relying on governments to regulate and control markets, we as consumers and investors need to rationally self-regulate ourselves in order to ensure that the market constantly moves in a positive direction and therefore all our assets and investments remain real (as opposed to inflated) and secure. As the 40th president of the United States, Ronald Regan once said "The nine most terrifying words in the English language are: I'm from the Government, and I'm here to help."

With that said, what even happened leading up to 2008 that created one of the largest financial bubbles in US history? The short answer is predatory lending practices that arose due to consumers overleveraging themselves in order to purchase properties and other assets they otherwise couldn't afford, essentially – greed. While typically the preceding sentence's underlying sentiment would cause mass protests and some readers may even be foaming at the mouth at the mere thought that the people and not the "mega corporations" ultimately caused the recession, hear me out.

The average house in 2007 (about a year before the crash) would have cost around $262,000. In 2022 that *same* house may cost $320,291. Of course, the average American does not have that much liquid capital to spend on a house, so what they do is apply for a mortgage loan on a house. In essence, people borrow money at an interest rate to pay for something they cannot afford outright. This isn't an issue, as a typical home buyer will put up/put down approximately 20-30% of the purchase price of a home, therefore for a $262,000 house, a typical down payment (assuming 20%) would be $52,400 and the bank/a lender would loan the home buyer the remaining sum ($209,600). This brings to light an interesting problem…" What if I don't have the money for a down payment, can I still buy the house? "Well in 2008, the answer was an excited YES! The reason this makes sense is that your monthly payment would be higher and so would your interest rate, therefore it is in the bank/lender's best interest that your down payment is as small as possible if it exists at all. This idea of "no money down, easy monthly payments" is classic predatory lending. We should never forget the old saying that states "there is no such thing as 'free money'".

With that said, if a good money-making opportunity for lenders and banks is to give out lots of home mortgages…why can't everyone have a mortgage? Well, sadly there are people with poor credit and those without a means to sustainably support themselves. The word credit is one that is thrown around a lot and can confuse people sometimes. So, what is credit?

Essentially credit is a measurement of someone's ability to repay loans on time. According to FICO (one of the major credit bureaus in the United States), aspects of credit include credit history, amounts owed, payment history, lines of new credit, and a credit mix. However, what if I told you that none of this prequalification mattered in '08 and that instead just so long as you can breathe and take up space a lender can guarantee you a mortgage, and not only can they get you one, but you don't have to pay anything upfront (no money down). This is, as Robert Kiyosaki would say, the "no money down, easy monthly payments" trap, which as mentioned earlier is classic predatory lending and a trademark of poor financial education (if you take the loan). Now, you might be asking yourself, "if the bank loans $262,000 to someone that they know won't be able to pay it off… How does the bank make money? Isn't this a dumb idea? ". Good question. The answer is that only the person that owns the debt is at a loss. Therefore, what the lenders did was they would sell the bad loans (also known as junk loans) to other banks/financial institutions at a premium, effectively cutting their ties and "making them whole again". The reason the debts (typically bundles of consumer/corporate debt) were sold at a premium is because the original lender "did all the work" and "found the customer" and so they charged for their ability to find customers. But why did the financial crisis happen? The owners of the bad debt eventually realized they were losing money on consumer debts they bought and as a result, those companies bled money, and some (such as Lehman Brothers) went bankrupt. Once the news got out that banks were "exploiting poor people" (as this kind of predatory lending effectively makes the poor even poorer) the government stepped in (notably former president Obama) and sought to remedy the issue. The problem lies in the question that people didn't ask. Was this issue really caused by those who filled the need or the person who had the need for money they couldn't repay? You see, under capitalist economic system consumers can make their own free decisions and so people who entered the predatory loans did it willingly, as no government forced them into these types of loans. Money is never free, and we all know that, but instead of saving, or buying a cheaper house people instead decided to spend money they didn't have. People's new and misguided hatred of banks went to Wallstreet quickly. People began pulling their money out of their investment accounts (many of which were managed by the institutions that people felt “screwed them over”) and as a result, there was a collapse in the economy. The government then spent billions of dollars and lots of time creating consumer protection laws and even going after many corporate executives at these banks because nobody wanted to admit that the root cause of this issue, just like the root cause of the 1930s recession wasn't the banks and institutions, it was consumer greed and over leveraging. The issue isn’t “mega-corporations”, and the root cause isn’t the government.

To expand on that a little further, the credit system was new in the 1920s and the 1930s. For the first time the idea of “buy now, pay later” came into play. People would buy things with money they would receive in the future because they wanted what they wanted today and were ok paying for it later. The issue then became that because people were becoming distanced from their money, the concept of monetary value was diminished and as a result, the nation went into massive amounts of debt. The problem began when the government adopted the idea of "buy now, pay later". While we didn't know then, nearly 100 years later the U.S. would try the same plan of "buying now and paying later" starting predominantly in the year 2020 (though the concept had been done before and even leading up to 2020). However, the term "by now, pay later" was and is *very* distasteful (mostly because of the great depression) and so we renamed this idea Quantitative Easing (a.k.a. QE). If we look at the following three recessions (including the one, we are in now) the fundamental issue is the notion that we can spend money now that we don't have on things that we want. Why can we do this? Oh, that's simple, we're just that awesome right? As Americans, we “deserve" everything we want and whether we have the means to get that which we want is irrelevant. We can always just print more money, right? That's what the Germans did during the Weimar inflation era. This sense of greed, and entitlement has caused at least three recessions in the U.S. and the concept has likewise tricked throughout the world and has existed throughout history.

To surmise this concept and sidestep what I believe to be the root cause we see people overextending themselves. Loans and leverage can be a powerful tool and they have built many million and even billion-dollar empires… but we need to be careful about the degree we extend ourselves.

The Credit Card Slave

How do banks and credit card companies consistently make money? Simple, they just try to turn their customers into perpetual debt slaves by incentivizing reckless spending. Yay eternal and generational poverty caused by a lack of basic financial education! Wait a minute… that's pretty messed up when you think about it. Essentially your buddies at the bank and credit card company want you to be in debt and they *don't* want to be paid back in full or on time. Why? To demonstrate "Credit Card Slavery" let's focus on a fictional character and his enslavement to the credit card. For arguments sake let's call him…. John Doe (the world's favorite generic guy). John works for a very typical company where he earns $54,000 a year (which is the

US average income at the time of writing this book). This means that (pretax) he makes $4,500 a month. John is a funny guy, he's 40 years old and rents out his childhood bedroom from his parents for $500 a month. Come on John, you can do better. Other than that, though, he has no other monthly expenses. With his remaining $4,000 a month John eats at nice restaurants every day, buys the newest tech, and goes out almost every weekend! You know John, he's a party animal! When he is asked to pay, he always says "oh., just put it on my card" and so all his expenses go on his credit card. At the end of the month however John receives a credit card bill for $5,000! Wait a minute, he made $4,000 after expenses but has a bill for $5,000? Well now John has a few options, he can either pay with his savings (if he has any) or he cannot pay the additional

$1,000 and leave it as a balance on his bill. If he does this however, he will be charged interest on the balance until he pays it off. “$1,000 dollars over? Oops' ' says John, “I’ll just pay it off next month”. A month goes by, and John only spends $4,500 this month. Now, he owes the $1,000 from last month, plus the interest on the balance, *plus* he also owes the $500 he overspent too. This cycle continues month over month and eventually John owes the credit card company $9,000. Credit card debt has a few aspects to focus on. The first (as was seen by John) is overspending even if by only a little every month. Any money not paid to the credit card company is charged interest, and the interest rates charged are *insane*! I’m talking about an insane 22.21% interest! This is practically predatory! To buy a house the average interest rate is around 6-7%, so the interest on a credit card debt is between 15-16% higher! The average credit card debt per household in the United States is currently around $9,00 and the total US credit card debt is somewhere between $887-$925 *billion*!

The problem starts when you overspend, then you are required to pay the balance plus interest. So, looking back at our buddy John Doe's situation after the first month his $1,000 balance became $1,220 and so while he might have budgeted for a $1,000 expense he didn't account for interest and so as a result he now owes $220 plus the amount (and interest on the amount) he overspent. This is how the cycle starts and once it starts it can be hard to break.

The Snowball Effect

There is this principle in finance called the "snowball effect". This effect works with debt and with wealth. As you can see with credit cards, the first missed payment or lack of paying in full creates a place for the interest to start creating bigger and bigger problems and then when you mix more overspending/over drafting in the mix the problem exponentially expands. One more detail I didn't mention, when you consistently don't pay in full and on time your credit score lowers. This is critical as this means that any and every time you need any kind of loan (e.g., car, personal, house, etc.) you *will* pay a significantly higher interest rate. So not only are you paying lots of money towards debt, but you are slowly creating the problem of raising your own interest rate on everything! Interest rates for people with poor credit is significantly higher than those with good or even excellent credit.

To demonstrate the difference in credit scores let's look at two people with vastly different credit scores trying to buy a house. One has excellent credit (800+) and the other has poor credit (620-639). The house they want to buy is an average two bed, and three-bathroom house in a decent part of town and it costs the average amount of money for a house in the US which is $348,000. They also both plan on making an average down payment which is 20% or $69,600. The person with excellent credit is told that he will have an interest payment of 6.826% on the $278,400 loan (ln). The loan officer apologizes and explains the high rate is because the economy is rough right now and the FED needs to raise interest rates. He then offers Mr. 800+ credit score some coffee, snacks and/or water while the bank finishes up the paperwork on his loan. What a kind lender! A+ customer service!! His monthly payment is $2,285 (including taxes). His friend however with the credit score between 620-639 will have an interest payment of 8.362% on the $278,400 loan if the bank will even lend him money at all, typically lenders look for a credit score of 740 or more. The loan officer will tell the borrower he is lucky they were able to get him a loan and that he will pay whatever they tell him and that he “better not be late on the monthly payment”. Then the loan officer hurriedly rushes Mr. 600’s out the door so they can talk to “more important clients' '. Maybe this loan officer isn’t that nice after all. I think we should complain on the internet to random people about him! 0 Stars! His monthly payment (with taxes and fees) will be around $2,578/mo. The person with poorer credit will be spending $293 per month for the same house. While $293 may seem like a small number, let's look at the difference over one year. The difference will be $3,516, and that is a decent chunk of change. What you must keep in mind too is banks and other lenders may not even lend to someone with a credit score in the 600's as they might be deemed "too risky".

As you can see, not only does the person with the higher credit score get better treatment, but he also saves more money purely by paying off his balance consistently every month as he has been for many months… years even.

Like said earlier, the snowball effect isn't limited to debt, and in fact can be used to become extremely wealthy. The snowball rolls both ways. To demonstrate the snowball rolling in a positive direction I'm going to introduce the stock market, which can be a very powerful tool (if used correctly). Even though there is a chapter dedicated to the stock market more in depth, here is one of the principles. When you buy stock (a part of a public company) sometimes there are dividends (also called yields) associated with the investment. Dividends are when a company pays you just for holding on to shares of stock. Typically, dividends are less than 5% and that 5% is broken up across the year into fiscal quarters. N.B not all companies are in the same fiscal calendar, so there is no one day where all companies pay dividends, they may be scattered. That said, let's look at an example of a stock market and dividend wealth snowball.

Adam Baker is a fresh college graduate, and he decides to start investing in this thing called the stock market because "all of the cool kids are doing it". Unlike his peers who are recklessly throwing money at meme coins, Adam decides to invest in stable companies with high dividend yields, and despite only having $500 to invest he knows his strategy will pay off largely in the future… if he plays his cards right. Adam finds three companies and buys $500 worth of shares across the three companies, in total he is expecting 9% ROI via dividends. At the end of the year, it turns out one of his company's raised dividends because the company was doing very well and so he was paid a total of 10% via dividends (or $50), in addition to this the value of his portfolio went from $500 to $600, however Adam decides not to sell and reinvests his earnings across the three companies again. Now he can expect to be paid dividends on the appreciation and on the dividend reinvestment. So as the stocks appreciated to $600, and he invested an additional $50 he can expect to be paid relative to $650. If he makes 10% per year in dividends as he did in the past and his portfolio appreciates by another $100, he will be going into year three with a portfolio valued at $815. Another very important thing to consider is Adam would most likely reinvest his earnings when he gets them instead of waiting until the end of the year so he can make money on his money. This snowball I am describing is known to many as "Compound Interest" which has been called "The eighth wonder of the world" by some random German guy named Albert Einstein. Personally, I was told not to take advice from strangers, but this German guy seems to be onto something.

The Stock Market

As promised, in this section I will cover the stock market. On May 17th, 1792, the Buttonwood agreement was signed in New York City establishing "The New York Stock Exchange" (NYSE). While in the eighteenth century they didn't have computers, nor the technology we have today, the core investment concepts are the same. There are a lot of different strategies to invest in the stock market and there are a lot of different markets as well. Besides international markets there are bond, commodity, crypto, and even debt markets to name a few. Plus, on top of that many of those markets have sub-categories such as treasury vs corporate bonds and in the commodity market there are metals, oil and natural gas. Uh-oh maybe you just learned something, sorry. But before I cover a few strategies you might use; it is important to know what the stock market is and a few key vocabulary words.

You could write hundreds if not thousands or more books on the stock market but who has the time for that? Instead, I'm going to focus on the basic and key concepts as ultimately that is what matters.

When you buy a stock, you are buying a portion of a publicly traded company. While there are lots of public companies there are also private companies that may or may not issue shares. While you can buy a stock at any price point the stock reaches, it is generally advised to "buy low" and "sell high". Companies can offer virtually an unlimited number of shares, and this leads us to the concept of dilution. Dilution is when the value of your stock is diminished (diluted) as more shares are offered to the public. An increase in the number of available shares of stock drives your “equity” down (the percentage of the company your shares represent). Facebook got in big trouble with one of its co-founders (Eduardo Saverin) over a dilution problem as was shown in the movie “The Social Network ". Specifically, what happened is Facebook (in order to grow) offered more and more shares to investors, but in order to protect his equity in the company CEO Mark Zuckerberg wrote in Facebook's corporate bylaws that his shares were not subject to dilution, however co-founder Eduardo Saverin’s shares were subject to dilution and as more shares were issued his stake in the company shrank. This is not uncommon nor is it illegal for certain corporate executives to be exempt from dilution, but such rules and exemptions must be in a corporation's bylaws. In order to simplify this a little more let's say hypothetically that Facebook offered 1,000 shares originally and Mark Zuckerberg controlled/owned 400 of those shares (40% equity) while his partner controlled 400 shares (40% equity) and therefore the publicly available shares was 200(20% of the total). Well as the company grew Facebook (in this example) decided to offer more shares to the public so they could raise more money. So, they issue new shares, let's say they issue an additional 1,000 shares such that now Facebook has a total of 2,000 shares that are to be accounted for. Zuckerberg (per the corporate bylaws) had and would remain in charge of 40% of the new shares or 800 shares. However, his partner (whose shares were subject to dilution) would maintain 400 shares, and therefore he went from controlling 40% of the company to 20% (in this example). Facebook and Zuckerberg (over time) eventually offered so many shares that Saverin eventually held less than a 1% stake in the company. Essentially Saverin was diluted out of Facebook.

Dilution and dividends (as dividends were covered earlier) aside, another important concept to understand as it relates to the stock market is options and options trading. Options trading is generally seen as very risky as you are predicting the future cost of 100 shares of a given stock, however they can be (if used correctly) a great tool. Some companies (such as Robinhood) have created covered options meaning they seize either money or stock in order to help mitigate risk in their behalf. That said there are two categories of options trading. A call is when you believe the value of a stock will increase in price/value relative to a set strike price, whereas a call is when you believe a stock will decrease in value relative to a set strike price. The key words here are the words ``strike price". Simply put a strike price is a fixed price at which a buyer can buy or sell a security/stock. In addition to determining the direction (up or down) a stock will go, in an options contract there is an expiration date. You can either make predictions that expire relatively soon (this is known as a short position), or you can make predictions on longer scales (known as going long). Before diving into and covering the four main types of options there are two more terms that you should be familiar with. Those are “in the money” and “out of the money” options. In The Money (ITM) options are options with a strike price that has already been passed by the current stock price. Conversely an Out of The Money (OTM) option has a strike price that the stock hasn’t reached yet.

That said, there are four main types of options you can execute, those four options are as follows: you can buy a put/call, or you can sell a put/call. Buying a call means you are paying a premium for the right to buy a security at a set price (the strike price) on or before a certain date in the future. Selling a call means that you are selling the obligation to purchase a security on or before a certain future date. I’m going to pause right here to cover a key differentiation that needs to be made. As mentioned in the last definition, there is a distinct difference between a right and an obligation to purchase or sell a security. The right to buy means that you can choose whether you do or do not want to execute the options contract at or by the expiration date. However, an obligation (as does arise in some options contracts, as we will soon see) requires the purchase or sale of a security on or before the expiration date. Buying a put means that you have the right to sell a security at a predetermined strike price. However, selling a put means that you have an *obligation* (as opposed to a right) to buy the security at a predetermined strike price from the option buyer *if they* exercise the option. Essentially buying either a call or put gives you a right to buy/sell respectively, and conversely a sell of an option requires you to be obligated to the sell provided the other party executes the contract.

Hopefully the paragraph above regarding options wasn’t too confusing, options have a stigma of being very confusing and messy and so if you're just starting out in the stock market or even if you have been in the market for many years, it might not be a bad idea to avoid options. In fact, if you're thinking “not only do I not want to get involved in betting the price of stocks in the future, but I don’t want to choose individual stocks to buy " Wall Street has just the solution for you. The solution to this problem is the different types of funds you can buy into. Specifically, I am referring to mutual and index funds. Index funds seek to make consistent, safe and reliable returns by investing across a wide variety of companies in many different sectors (depending on the fund). A very common example of an index fund is the S&P 500 which is a collection of the 500 biggest US companies. However, unlike index funds, mutual funds are more actively managed and are intended to outperform the market by taking riskier positions. However, since mutual funds require more active management, the fees (e.g., management fees) are typically higher than the low (or nonexistent) fees of an index fund. Additionally, since mutual funds are focused on outperforming the market (and therefore take riskier bets) they sometimes underperform the market. The company Black Rock is one of the largest mutual funds in the world with approximately $10 trillion AUM (Assets Under Management) as of January of 2022. However, as famous investor and

Berkshire Hathaway CEO and Chairman Warren Buffet once said, “In my view, for most people, the best thing to do is owning (shares) (of) the S&P 500 index fund”. That said, it is ultimately up to the investor to decide where to place their money. The stock market truly is an ocean of opportunity.

Debt: The Good, Bad and the Stupid

Changing gears now, I wanted to dedicate a section of this book to debt. In a previous chapter I talked about credit card debt and the vicious poverty cycle. However, what I want to mention is that contrary to what society tells you about debt, not all debt is bad. As I see it there are three categories of debt, there is good debt, bad debt and stupid debt. But what makes debt good, bad or stupid?

Stupid debt is money that you owe on things that don't produce monetary or real value. An example of stupid debt is credit card debt, because you are paying interest on money that you overspent, and you may end up like our friend John who was beginning to get himself into a vicious cycle of poverty. Basically, stupid debt costs you money to be in debt.

Bad debt is money owed on something that cash flows negative. A typical example of bad debt (and Dave Ramsay would love to hear this) *can* be the debt on a personal car loan. Car debt is bad because in addition to paying interest on the car itself and paying for something that is constantly costing you more money, the car is also constantly losing value. In fact, a car loses between 9-11% of its value the second you drive it off the lot. Calling car debt bad debt is lenient, but the reason I have classified it as bad debt rather than stupid debt is because in most places in the US you legitimately need a car. However, uber, carpooling, public transportation and walking are also always options.

Time for the good news! Good debt is money that you owe on something that is making you more money than the debt payment. A classic example of good debt is the debt owed via a mortgage on an *investment* property. Say for instance your monthly mortgage payment on a house is $1,000/mo however you rent the house out for $2,500/mo, let's also presuppose that after all your expenses are paid you are left with $200/mo in profit. What you can see is that although you are technically in debt, because you are cash flow positive (aka "in the black") you are getting paid and making a profit on being in debt. Therefore, since you are making money, this type of debt *can* be a good thing.

Something important I want to clarify is that the terms "good" "bad" and "stupid" debt is all relative. To demonstrate this let's look at one of the types of debt that many Americans run into early in their adult lives…student debt. Student debt can be a form of stupid debt, but it can also be good debt, it really depends. Student debt is one of, if not the only type of debt that will stick with you until you die, and then it will be passed on if it's not paid. "What if I declare personal bankruptcy" the answer is the student loan stays with you. In the case you declare bankruptcy to dodge student debt, not only would you have failed to "dodge the bullet" but now your credit score would be messed up. If you remember back from earlier, your credit score is a verry, verry, verry, verry, verry, verry very important number.

If you take out student debt that helps you get paid more than you otherwise would, that *can* be a good idea...*but* <u>it depends</u> on how much more it can make you. Let's say you take out $25,000 dollars' worth of student loans and by taking out $25,000 of student loans you calculate that you could make $100 more dollars a year than someone that doesn't have a college degree. Is it worth taking out ten thousand dollars to make $100 more a year? Probably not. However, if you take out $25,000 in student loans in order to make $100,000 more a year than if you didn't have a degree then *maybe* taking the loan would be a good idea. "Why did you say maybe it would be a good idea? One hundred thousand dollars is a lot of money". Well, yes, one hundred thousand dollars is a lot of money but what happens if you take out the twenty-five-thousand-dollar loan, then decide to change majors? Or even worse what happens if you drop out? Did you know that by 2022 40% of undergraduate students dropped out of college? Given this example you would now have $25,000 of non-bankrupt able student loans, and no degree. Did I mention the loan also has interest? In fact, currently US federal student loans are around 5%. So, if you had $25,000 dollars of student loan debt, with a 5% interest rate and paid the average monthly payment of $234/mo it would take you 112 months (around 9 years) to pay off your debt. Now, you might be saying "$25,000 of student loan debt? That's a crazy number. Are you high !?". You know… you're right, that is a low number. The actual average amount of student debt in 2022 is about $37,787. So, if we assume the same minimum monthly payment and interest rate it would take 170 months (about 14 years) to pay off *if* you pay on time and every month. Remember what happens when you don't make your credit card payment on time? They throw on a big interest rate on the balance you didn't pay (e.g., 22%), fortunately (now) late payment interest rates are 6% of the balance, but… (and you're going to love this) *it depends* on your lender. There is nothing stopping the bank from giving you a "poor persons tax" of a large interest rate on the balance of outstanding student loan debt.

I hope this chapter hasn't depressed you completely, the good news is that debt can be a powerful tool for building wealth, but like I said and as you can see it can also destroy and doom you. It just depends on what side of the "snowball" you're on. I would recommend being on the side that is making money…but hey… you do you.

How To Build Wealth

I have spent a lot of time in this book going over what not to do and things to avoid and be aware of, but I haven't talked a lot about what to do. So, I figure "you know, this is towards the end of the book, why not have some suggestions (but not official or legal financial advice)". So here we go.

Like I said in the introduction to this book it has always been a plan and a goal of mine to become extremely wealthy. I plan on doing this by renting out real estate and by investing in the stock market. Yes, that's a generic answer, so let me elaborate more. I want to spend most of my time and energy in the real estate game because by using leverage and good debt I see the most amount of practically guaranteed return and even then, I will always own a physical product which will always have some degree of intrinsic value. However, except for major news events and their influence of the stock market (which as a good capitalist I plan to use to my advantage, as we all should) I see the stock market as a better savings account than the typical bank. Traditionally the stock market grants a 10% annual return to investors, whereas banks pay their customers less than 1% interest on the money placed in a bank account. That said, I'm not saying having no money in the bank is a good idea. It is a good idea to have an emergency fund and some liquid cash on hand (in case you need it for something). However, I plan on storing lots of money in the stock market plus I can try and legally avoid taxes that way too, which is always a good idea. The key here is getting out of taxes legally. As the old saying goes there are three things certain in life: death, taxes and an end to this book.

There truly are seemingly limitless ways to make money, both legally and uhh…otherwise. However, because there are so many extraordinary opportunities to make money legally, it would be foolish and extremely risky to try to make money illegally. For me however, I believe the stock market and real estate should (to some degree) be in everyone's portfolio. Approximately 90% of the world's millionaires are (to some degree) invested in real estate. Don’t reinvent the wheel, invest in real estate…but be careful how you do it. In the first chapter of this book, I briefly covered the 2008 recession in the US caused by the idea of “easy, free and cheap money" and well, the effects of the 2008 recession are still trickling through the US and even global economy today.

Although as you can tell from the table of contents our time together is coming to an end, I want to tell you one big money secret that rich people obsess about. What is the secret? Two words. Cash Flow.

Two Words. Cash Flow.

Think about your money and your income like a river. Every month when you receive your paycheck what do you do with it? Do you follow a written budget? Well statistically…probably not. In fact, only about 41% of American households prepare a budget (as of 2016), and do you honestly think that 100% of that 41% completely follow their budget to the penny? No. The good news is the secret of cash flow is completely focused on saving (although saving is important) but rather cashflow it's focused on where your money is going.

One of my favorite Robert Kiyosaki quotes is "It's not how much money you make, but how much money you keep, how hard it works for you, and how many generations you keep it for.". You see it's not how much you make that makes you wealthy, but it's how much you keep and how your money works for you. When you get your paycheck, each month do you spend it all? If you, do it do matter how much you make, because in the end you're left with nothing. Retirement is going to be hard, even with social security if you spend all your money. But again, wealth is how much you keep (don't spend) and how hard *your money works for you.* Like I pointed out earlier, money sitting in the bank can make less than 1% interest per year, versus money in the stock market (generally) making around 10% which is a significantly better ROI (Return on Investment). If instead of funneling your money (or flowing) your money into things that lose you money, if you take charge of and redirect the flow into things that generate more money (e.g., real estate, businesses, etc.) you will be much better served in the long run. Plus, money is like a snowball (and it is) than your investments are worth significantly more than they are when you buy them. Why? They help add to your wealth snowballs momentum, that is a part of the true value of cash flow. Being able to control the cash flow river and your own wealth and/or debt snowball is what truly wealthy people can do. The good news is that you're at least more aware of what's going on now. Approximately one third of the US population is not fiscally literate, and this is a real problem as those are the kinds of people that are getting run over by the debt snowball and are ending up in these rough financial situations. In fact, you probably know many people in your life that aren't financially literate. Let's hope though that they can read books though, specifically this one (insert selfless self-promotion here). To those readers who got this book as a gift from someone they know…. don't worry I'm not talking about you….

Conclusion

I don't think I've used bullet points in this book yet, and because it's better to read to entire book to understand the context of this chapter. So, I'm going to use bullet points to drive home a couple of key concepts from across this book, if you want more information go back to the chapter where the material was covered, you already paid for the content.

- Money isn't free, cheap or easy. Sorry, it just isn't.
- Credit cards (and the credit system) can be very beneficial *if* you pay on time and in full every time.

- Credit Card companies (and banks) want you to be in debt, don't be in bad or stupid debt to them.

- Money is like a snowball, it has momentum and said momentum can propel you towards massive wealth, or extreme poverty. Therefore, it's in your best interest to take control of your snowball.
- The Stock market is a large, old and powerful tool. Don't treat the stock market like a casino and gamble away all your money. Play the game right.
- The stock market is much more than buying and selling stock (stake in) a company.
- Not all debt is bad, but some debt is stupid.
- The difference between good, bad and stupid debt *depends* on the context.
- Cashflow is a huge part of the money snowball, when you control it, you control your financial life.

- When you control your finances, you truly control your life.
- The End.

www.ingramcontent.com/pod-product-compliance
Lightning Source LLC
LaVergne TN
LVHW080458160826
845677LV00006B/1403

9798366529884